This book belongs to :

Timmy the Whale likes to count to thirty

ISBN-10: 0692999574
ISBN-13: 978-0692999578

Dedicated to my son Gunnar

Timmy the whale likes to count to thirty. But sometimes he forgets some of the numbers.

Timmy would like you to help.

Timmy's favorite thing to count is the fish that jump out of the water.

Can you help Timmy the whale
count thirty fish ?

Great!

Do you see the fish jumping ?

Let's start to count the fish now.

Timmy knows this one. It's how old he is going to be , but he can't remember. Lets give him a little help. Do you know the number?

Six ! Yes, six! Timmy remembers now.

Timmy sees more fish jumping . Let's keep counting.

Timmy forgot what's after nine.

Can you help?

If you said ten, your right !
Ten is the missing number.

There are more fish jumping . Let's count with Timmy.

Timmy needs help.

What's after fourteen ?

If you said fifteen, your right ! Fifteen is after fourteen.

15

Let's keep counting.

15  **16**  **17**  **18**

19

Timmy is thinking . What comes after nineteen ?

Twenty ! Timmy remembers.

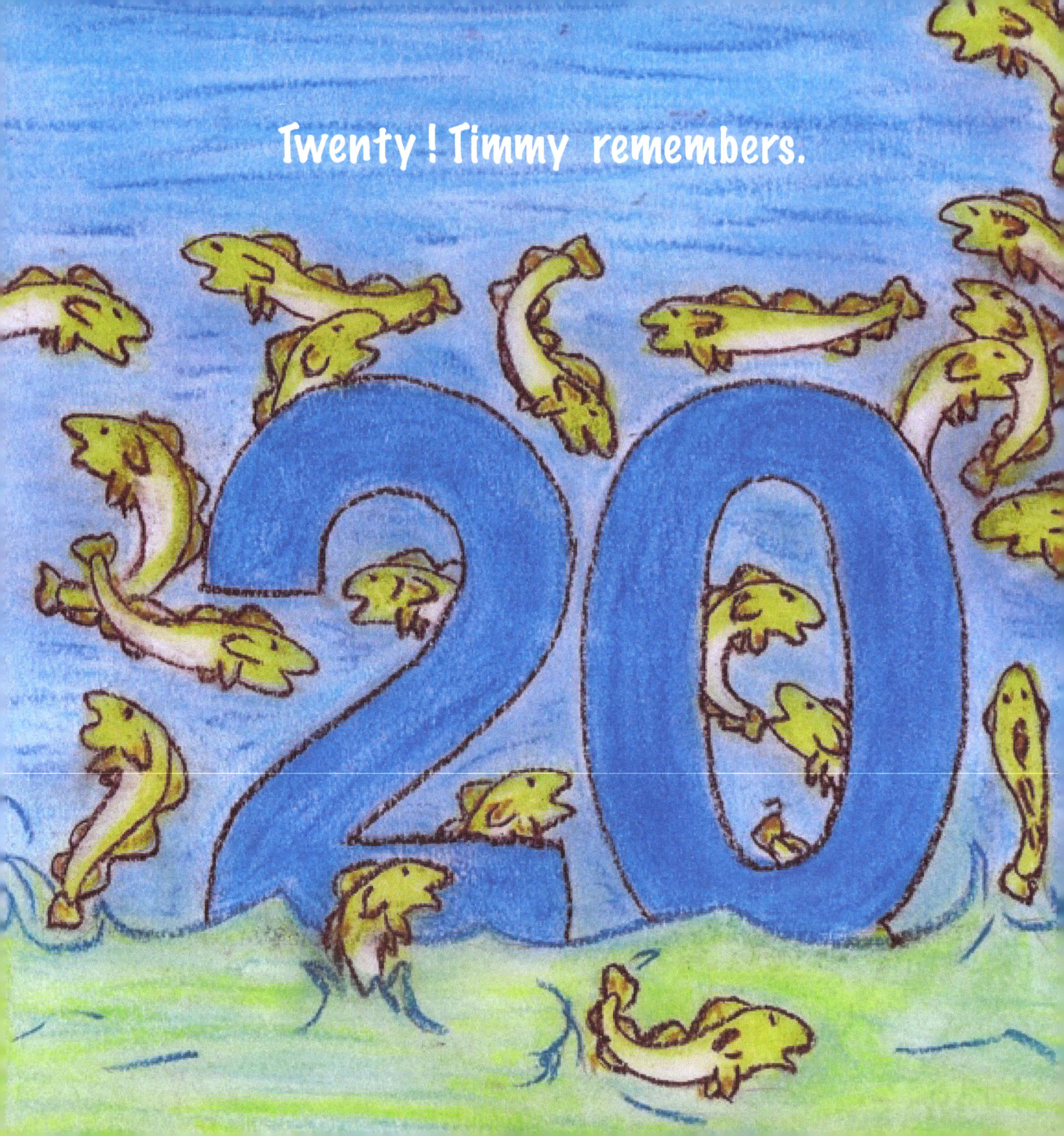

Did you remember too ?

Now, let's keep counting.

1 2 3 4 5 6

12 13 14 15

20 21 22

Oh no ! Timmy forgot what comes after twenty five .

25 ___

Can you help him ?

If you said twenty six, your right! The number twenty six was the missing number.

We are almost to Timmy's favorite number. So lets keep counting.

1 2 3 4 5

11 12 13 14

19 20 21 22

26 27 28 29

Oh no ! Timmy forgot his favorite number.

What do you think it is ? Can you help?

If you said thirty, your right ! Thirty is Timmy's favorite number.

Timmy is so happy you helped him count to thirty.

Write your favorite number that is over thirty here and see if you can count that high.

Timmy knows you can.

www.ingramcontent.com/pod-product-compliance
Lightning Source LLC
LaVergne TN
LVHW072055070426
835508LV00002B/101